The Majesty of
MOBILE

Mobile's waterfront skyline is dominated by the thirty-five-story RSA Battlehouse Tower and RSA Bank Trust Building.

Raphael Semmes was the famed captain of the Confederate cruiser CSS Alabama. His statue, on Government Street, is engraved with "Sailor, Patriot, Statesman and Scholar."

RAPHAEL SEMMES

← P
Convention Center
State Docks
Int'l. Trade Ctr.

The Majesty of
MOBILE

Text by Jim Fraiser
Photography by Pat Caldwell
Foreword by John Sledge

PELICAN PUBLISHING COMPANY

GRETNA 2012

Library of Congress Cataloging-in-Publication Data

Fraiser, Jim, 1954-
  The majesty of Mobile / text by Jim Fraiser ; photography by Pat Caldwell
; foreword by John Sledge.
    p. cm.
  ISBN 978-1-4556-1491-2 (hardcover : alk. paper) — ISBN 978-1-
4556-1492-9 (e-book) 1. Architecture—Alabama—Mobile. 2. Historic
districts—Alabama—Mobile. 3. Mobile (Ala.)—Buildings, structures,
etc. I. Caldwell, Pat (James Patrick), 1957- II. Title.
  NA735.M62F73 2012
  720.9761'22—dc23
                                        2011039087

*Page 3: Fort Conde has been partially reconstructed at 150 South Royal Street.
The fort's brick walls and cannon held sway over Mobile for 100 years in service
of the French, British, Spanish, and Americans.*

Printed in China
Published by Pelican Publishing Company, Inc.
1000 Burmaster Street, Gretna, Louisiana 70053

For my son, Paul—J. F.

Battleship Memorial Park features the World War II-era battleship USS Alabama.

Architecture is my delight . . . worth great attention. It is then, among the most important arts. Were I to tell you how much I enjoy . . . architecture, sculpture, painting, music, I should want words.

—Thomas Jefferson

This I regard as history's highest function, to let no worthy action be uncommemorated, and to hold out the reprobation of posterity as a terror to evil words and deeds.

—Tacitus

Contents

Foreword	9
Acknowledgments	11
CHURCH STREET EAST HISTORIC DISTRICT	15
Bishop Portier House	15
Barton Academy	19
Hall-Ford House	20
Government Street Presbyterian Church	21
Christ Episcopal Church	23
Waring Texas House	27
Chandler House	28
Fort Conde-Charlotte House	29
Chamberlain-Rapier House	36
Kennedy House	38
Admiral Semmes House	39
Hallett House	40
Spear House	41
Tardy Cottage	42
Guesnard House	43
Hamilton House	47
Big Zion A.M.E. Church	48
Ketchum House	50
Frohlichstein/Goldsmith Houses	51
Horst House	56
Pollock House	58
LOWER DAUPHIN HISTORIC DISTRICT	59
Cathedral of the Immaculate Conception	59
DETONTI SQUARE HISTORIC DISTRICT	64
Hunter-King House	64
Beal-McNeal House	65
Turner Cottage	66
Parmly Houses	67
Gee-Pugh House	69
St. John House	70
Richards House	71
Lyon House	77
Butt-Kling House	78
Bush-Sands Memorial	80
OAKLEIGH GARDEN HISTORIC DISTRICT	82
Oakleigh Place	82
Cox-Deasy House	86
Rapelje-Delaney House (Landmark Hall)	88

Hellen House   94
Goelete-Randlette House   95
Roberts-Abbott House   96
Joe Cain House   97
Twelve Oaks (Smith-Cutts House)   99
Kilduff House   100
Bennett House   101
Blacksher Hall   102
Forcheimer-Burke-Helmer House   107
Tacon-Gordon-Tissington-Vitalo House   108
Burgess-Maschmeyer House   111
OLD DAUPHIN WAY HISTORIC DISTRICT   113
Vincent House   113
Gates-Daves House   116
Macy House   117
Monterey Place   119
MIDTOWN HISTORIC DISTRICT   122
Carlen House   122
Georgia Cottage   123
Bragg-Mitchell House   125
Sacred Heart Chapel   128
SPRING HILL NEIGHBORHOOD   131
Collins-Robinson House   131
Beal-Galliard House   132
Carolina Hall   133
Stewartfield   135
Marshall-Eslava-Hixon-Dixon House   137
Palmetto Hall   138
Saint Paul's Episcopal Chapel   139
ASHLAND PLACE HISTORIC DISTRICT   140
Waterman House   140
LEINKAUF HISTORIC DISTRICT   141
Chamberlain House   141
DOWNTOWN   142
Caravello House   142
MARTIN LUTHER KING, JR. AREA   143
Dave Patton House   143
DAPHNE   144
Adams-Stone House   144

Foreword

A book such as this has long been overdue, namely, a celebration in stunning color photographs and readable prose of the glorious architecture, both grand and modest, that lines the oak-canopied streets of Mobile, Alabama. Locals and visitors have always known about Mobile's rich architectural legacy, of course—one antebellum traveler declared the city the most distinctive he had seen, a sentiment echoed by Pres. Woodrow Wilson during his 1913 visit—but until now there hasn't been a suitably attractive and accessible volume communicating that to take home, display, and thumb through with such pleasure. Readers of this book who know Mobile will more than likely experience a clutch of the heart within these pages, and those who don't will likely be making travel plans as soon as possible.

So what is it that makes Mobile's built environment so special? After all, many other towns have monumental Greek Revival churches, elegant Italianate houses, polychromatic Queen Anne mansions, and cozy bungalows. Granted, these are all national styles, but when encountered on a Mobile street overarched by live oak trees, flanked by azalea bushes, and lined with cast-iron lampposts, they seem somehow sprung uniquely from this sandy soil, to be lovingly caressed by just these salty breezes. And then there are the Creole and Gulf Coast cottages, more vernacular expressions that trace their pedigree back to the Caribbean and then to Normandy. Often effortlessly blended with more formal architectural expressions such as Greek Revival, these lovely cottages are defined by their strong side-gabled profiles and full recessed (and sometimes wraparound) porches—or *galleries,* as the French colonists termed them. Mobile's porches are some of the South's most inviting, in fact, and play no small role in imparting a small-town charm to a city that is actually much larger than many unsuspecting observers might guess.

Though founded more than three hundred years ago, Mobile, alas, can no longer boast any of its earliest architecture or, for that matter, too many landmark structures from all the subsequent decades. These buildings—the original protective fort, a wooden Catholic church, timber and mud dwellings with tile or, more likely, palmetto-frond roofs, and a long list of jaw-dropping houses and churches and stores—are vanished, done in either by the hot, wet climate or such vagaries as storm, fire, war, and neglect.

It's hard to say for sure when Mobilians began to realize just how important the buildings crowding so familiarly all around them might be. No one appears to have batted an eye, for example, when the bricks of old Fort Conde were pulled down by energetic Americans during the 1820s and used for fill along the Mobile River's marshy banks. By their lights, the fort was an antiquated pile, no longer necessary for defense in the brash and growing young Republic, and besides it was in the way. Room needed to be made for streets, offices, houses, stores, taverns, and, critical to antebellum wheeling and dealing, coffeehouses. Opinion had turned a bit by 1895, however, when the Old Guard House (erected in 1839) with its distinctive clock tower was torn down to build the (now lost too) German Relief Hall. A writer for the *Mobile Commercial Register* noted the demolition in somewhat wistful terms. "The antique-looking building," he wrote, "formerly occupied by the police authorities and behind the massive walls of which so many have pined in durance vile, [is] no more."

The 1930s, '40s, and '50s saw a flowering of local colorists, people such as Marian Acker MacPherson, William and Annie Shillito Howard, Genevieve Southerland, S. Blake McNeely, and Caldwell Delaney, whose etchings, paintings, photographs, poetry, and prose alluringly conjured the city's romantic past, especially as manifested in its architecture. Moss-hung trees foregrounding gently decaying brick townhouses; ornate, rusting cast-iron gates; columned mansions reduced to surplus stores or vacancy; and colorful contextual figures, usually African American, sporting fishing poles or laundry bundles were their stock in trade. These buildings, they were saying through their creative works, mostly overlooked amid the hurly-burly, were the past made tangible, and worthy of preservation. Short on scholarship as much of this material was, it nonetheless paved the way for successful historic-homes tours and heritage organizations such as the Historic Mobile Preservation Society, Friends of Magnolia Cemetery, and the Mobile Historic Development Commission, which have done much to raise awareness and fight for what remains of historic Mobile.

Too often, we preservationists and not a few longtime inhabitants decry what has already been lost in Mobile—the remarkable rows of three-, four-, and five-story riverfront saloons and warehouses, the Southern Hotel, St. John's Episcopal Church, the LeVert House, the United States Customs House, the Scattergood-Grey House, Bloodgood Row, and whole neighborhoods of shotgun houses and side-hall cottages leveled during Urban Renewal. But as this beautiful book makes clear, much else remains as a feast for the eye and the imagination. There is, for example, the Cathedral of the Immaculate Conception with its soaring, gilded towers and barrel-vaulted interior; Christ Episcopal Church with its highly formal Greek Revival façade and priceless Tiffany windows; the Hall-Ford House with its masterful mix of Creole and classical elements; Georgia Cottage with its famous literary associations and long oak alley; the Marshall-Eslava-Hixon-Dixon House with its intact antebellum garden; and the Kilduff House with its flat-sawn balustrade and palmettos in the yard. Indeed, whether you are Old Mobile or a tourist from Honolulu, Hoboken, Hampshire, Herat, or anywhere else, these pages will surely delight and instruct. Enjoy.

—John Sledge

Acknowledgments

I gratefully acknowledge the assistance of the staff at the Mobile Historic Development Commission, especially that of author John Sledge, whose expertise on Mobile was vital to the successful completion of this project. I also appreciate the early guidance of former Mobilians Kathryn Day Watkins and Lucy Duffy Tankersley and the editing of Nina Kooij. Our endless thanks go to the owners of the lovely houses we covered in this book, and those responsible parties at the churches and museums we visited, for graciously allowing us in their private and public spaces and taking the time to share them with us.

Herd Records, at the corner of Dauphin and Dearborn, celebrates Mobile music with this colorful mural on its exterior studio brick wall. The mural was painted by local artist Brian Young.

Messages of wit and wisdom cover the walls of the original Wintzell's Oyster House. Founded in 1938 by Oliver Wintzell at 605 Dauphin Street, it is a perennial Mobile favorite for locals and tourists alike.

The Majesty of
MOBILE

Mobile is known as the City of Six Flags, for the flags that have flown over it—the French king flag, the British Union Jack, the Spanish flag, the U.S. flag, the Republic of Alabama flag of 1861, and the flag of the Confederate States of America.

Church Street East Historic District

Bishop Portier House
307 Conti Street

This one-and-a-half-story Gulf Coast cottage constructed of handhewn timbers was erected circa 1834 at a cost of about seven thousand dollars to serve as the home of Michael Portier, the first bishop of Mobile and father of Spring Hill College, who described it as "an honorable residence and a handy one." Fr. Abraham Ryan, the Confederacy's "poet-priest," lived here in the 1870s, and it served as the bishop's dwelling until 1914. Restored in 1958 as a private residence, its design is attributed to French seminarian Claude Beroujon. Although the type is five-bay cottage with Creole-style casement windows, the detailing is classical style, with a Federal pilastered entrance framed by a transom and sidelights, entablature, narrow architrave, and frieze embellished with triglyphs and metopes; a Tuscan-columned gallery; and segmental arched dormers with denticulation and curved upper lights.

Listed in the Historic American Buildings Survey, this house shares the same original designer as that of the first Spring Hill College Administration Building and the interior of the body of the Cathedral of the Immaculate Conception, although the latter was substantially altered over time. It is now open to the public.

The box grand piano, circa 1840, is made of rosewood with mother-of-pearl inlay, a scroll-carved music rack, and several remaining ivory keys.

The staircase features arrow-shaped balusters.

Bishop Portier House has beautiful fireplace mantels.

A chandelier suspends from an elaborate medallion.

Barton Academy
504 Government Street

Renowned architects James Gallier, Sr., and James and Charles B. Dakin designed this Greek Revival-style public-school building in 1836 as the brainchild of Alabama legislator Willoughby Barton. Substantial funding came from Alabama's "first millionaire" and first state attorney general, Judge Henry Hitchcock, as well as from taxes on "spirituous liquor, bear baiting, bullfighting and pool rooms." The two-story façade features a gabled monumental hexastyle Ionic portico, flanked by projecting pilastered bays. The brick walls are stuccoed and scored to resemble stone, and the dome rests on an Ionic-colonnaded rotunda. All of these elements are indicative of the style that was popular during that era for statehouses and other grand public structures. Originally occupied by four separate tuition and denominational schools, the building subsequently served as a free public school, a Civil War hospital, again a school, and finally the home of the Board of School Commissioners. It is currently vacant.

Barton Academy was placed in the National Register of Historic Places in 1970 and is listed in the Historic American Buildings Survey. It was renovated in 1969-70.

Hall-Ford House
165 St. Emmanuel Street

This 9,000-square-foot, two-and-a-half-story, five-bay, center-hall house was built in 1836 for commission merchant and eventual Mobile mayor Edward Hall, a native Philadelphian. It features a rare masonry first floor, scored with stucco to simulate ashlar, and a frame-clapboard second level. The two-story, front-elevation gallery is supported by six brick and plaster Doric columns below and six wood Doric columns above. Fluted pilasters frame the ends of the first-story gallery, and the dormers are pedimented. All doors are fitted with Carpenter locks, each with a small brass "penny" inserted on the lock's face.

The substantially remodeled Hall-Ford House features an original rear-elevation courtyard, rear ell, and a two-story brick servant's quarters.

Government Street Presbyterian Church
300 Government Street

Reminiscent of a classical Greco-Roman temple, with a massive denticulated triangular pediment and brick walls scored to resemble stone, the Government Street Presbyterian Church was erected in 1836 for around sixty thousand dollars. It was designed by architects James Gallier and Charles Dakin and constructed by mason Thomas James. The distinctive recessed porch utilizes a distyle-in-antis plan, with Ionic columns between end bays with large box pilasters. The interior is distinguished by a deeply coffered diamond-pattern ceiling, a main-auditorium three-sided balcony with columns similar to those used in Athens' Tower of Winds (40 B.C.), side molding with Greek key design, and, behind the pulpit, four Corinthian columns supporting an entablature with rosettes and denticulation.

The Government Street Presbyterian Church, one of the least-altered Greek Revival church buildings in America, was designated a National Historic Landmark in 1994.

The main auditorium features a deeply coffered diamond-pattern ceiling and a pipe organ occupying the full rear balcony.

Christ Episcopal Church
114 St. Emmanuel Street

This Greek Revival-style temple was begun in 1838 by architects Fredrick Bunell and Cary Butt and builder James Barnes on the site of Mobile's first Protestant church. Louisiana diocesan bishop Leonidas Polk, the future Confederate general, consecrated it in 1840. The structure features twelve-foot-thick foundation walls, a distyle-in-antis façade with fluted Greek Doric columns, an entablature with classically spaced metopes and triglyphs in the frieze, flanking side-bay pilasters, a north-elevation stained-glass window depicting Christ's baptism, and two Tiffany stained-glass windows.

Christ Episcopal Church was severely damaged by a 1906 hurricane, which destroyed a Wren-Gibbs steeple with Greek Revival detailing of distyle-in-antis Doric columns underneath a first-level entablature and a third-level cupola.

The stained-glass portrayal of Jesus' baptism, by D'Ascenzo Studios of Philadelphia, is located above an 1840 marble baptismal font.

In this window by Franz Mayer Company in Munich, Jesus blesses the children.

This stained-glass window depicts New Testament scenes.

This window honors the SPCA.

Waring Texas House
110 South Claiborne Street

The one-and-a-half-story building known as Waring Texas has a history and architecture as unique as its name. John Nugent constructed it in 1840 as an outbuilding to the main house on Government Street. Moses Waring purchased it in 1868 to convert it into a *garçonnière* for his sons. The main house was demolished in the 1940s. This building later served as a schoolhouse and headquarters for a mystic society. The Greek Revival style is evident in the simple box columns, light entablature, and unadorned side gable, fashioned in the Charleston side-entrance plan with a fenestrated short end on the street and gallery accessible through a privacy fence.

Waring Texas, listed in the Historic American Buildings Survey, derives its name from being separated from the main house, just as the Republic of Texas was separated from the United States.

Chandler House
205 Church Street

    This two-story, three-bay brick townhouse has classical elements in its rectangular shape, offset right wing, and raised-parapet end walls, although the Italianate three-bay, cast-iron porch with balustraded deck is a subsequent addition. Built in 1844 for Daniel Chandler, this structure was formerly attached to another on its west side that was demolished by Hurricane Frederic's 1979 rampage. The classical-style façade is stuccoed, with a single-leaf entrance door framed by paneled pilasters, and double-hung sashes with six-over-nine lights. Curving cast-iron steps lead to the side porch.

The Chandler House is currently a law office. It is located in the Church Street Historic District, which was listed in the National Register of Historic Places in 1971.

Fort Conde-Charlotte House
104 Theater Street

This Greek Revival-style, side-gable house, with stuccoed-brick Tuscan pillars below and a wood Corinthian-columned gallery with crow's-foot balustrade above, is also known as the Kirkbride House. New Jersey native and banker/builder Jonathan Kirkbride, along with Robert Ellis, erected it in 1845 to include a wall from an adjacent jail built in 1822. The jail had been built on the foundations of Fort Conde, and some relics remain. Kirkbride and Ellis added a second-floor gallery and east wing in 1849-50, and the house became the Kirkbride family residence in 1853. Restored in 1940 by the Historic Mobile Preservation Society, it is now a public museum owned by the National Society of Colonial Dames in the State of Alabama, with rooms decorated with eighteenth- and nineteenth-century antiques.

The Fort Conde-Charlotte House was listed in the National Register of Historic Places in 1973.

29

The flags of former ruling governments fly from the balcony. Each regime is remembered in rooms beautifully furnished with period antiques.

A portion of the jail foundation, as seen from the museum floor, shows a brass-ring shackle.

The authentically equipped kitchen features a fireplace, a brick floor, and even a jail-cell door.

The back wooden balcony offers a view of the walled formal Spanish garden and the double brick walls of Fort Conde in the background.

An original French Fort Conde cannon rests in the front yard of the house.

The Confederate parlor contains a period organ.

The French sitting room includes a George Washington portrait, Chippendale writing table circa 1765, and Chippendale secretary circa 1770.

The dining room features a convex Federal mirror with a carved eagle on top, circa 1815.

The French parlor features a rosewood sleigh bed (or Greek loveseat).

35

Chamberlain-Rapier House
56-58 South Conception Street

This brick double house was constructed in 1852 by Henry Chamberlain and Judge Charles W. Rapier, and the latter and his descendants resided here from 1856 to 1946. A high arched masonry carriageway divides the structure and originally led to stables beyond. Classical elements include a low gable roof, cornice with dentil course, deeply recessed entrances framed by Tuscan pilasters and featuring slightly pedimented lintels and battered jambs, six-over-six lights, and eight cast-iron posts supporting a second-story iron rail.

The Chamberlain-Rapier House was listed in the Historic American Buildings Survey and features a rare original carriageway.

This arched brick carriageway separates the two addresses here, leading from Conception Street to the rear of the two-sided structure.

Kennedy House
607 Government Street

Indian interpreter Thomas Price sold his Spanish land grants on this site to William and Joshua Kennedy, Jr., who owned much of downtown Mobile at the time. Joshua erected this two-story, three-bay, stuccoed-brick townhouse with Italianate elements in 1857, with four monumental Tuscan columns supporting a portico with flattened arches, semicircular-headed windows, and bracketed eaves. The remaining cast-iron fence is of acorn-and-leaf design. The Kennedy descendants resided here until 1923, after which it served as the Seaman's Bethel for twenty years. The American Legion Post #3 then restored the building, receiving the first Architectural Award from the Historic Mobile Preservation Society in 1950. It has since fallen into disrepair.

The Kennedy House was listed in the Historical American Buildings Survey in 1963.

Admiral Semmes House
802 Government Street

This two-story, three-bay, Federal-style masonry townhouse was erected in 1859. It features a gable roof between raised-end parapet walls, recessed entrance decorated with Doric pilasters, flat-headed windows, and a one-story cast-iron gallery surmounted by a balustrade of floral pattern and centered by a cluster of three lilies (added in the 1870s). The citizens of Mobile purchased the house in 1871 for donation to Adm. Raphael Semmes, commanding officer of the sloop of war CSS *Alabama* and popular lawyer, judge, and newspaper editor in Mobile. This famous Confederate raider captured sixty-nine prizes in the Caribbean and Atlantic on his way to becoming the only North American to hold the ranks of brigadier general and rear admiral simultaneously. Mr. and Mrs. J. L. Bledsole restored the house in 1946 and donated it to the First Baptist Church in memory of their son, Lt. J. L. Bledsole, Jr.

The Admiral Semmes House was listed in the National Register of Historic Places in 1970.

Hallett House
503 Government Street

William Hallett, cotton merchant, Bank of Mobile director, and owner of the Lafayette Hotel, built this two-story, brick-bearing, wood-frame townhouse in 1859 in the Italianate style. It features a bracketed cornice overhang, first-level arched cast-iron gallery, second-story railing, chimneys capped by terracotta flues, and double-hung sashes with two-over-two lights (not original). However, the square-headed windows and recessed entrance with Doric pilasters and rectangular sidelights and transom constitute Greek Revival elements.

Hallett House features a rare surviving (for Mobile) flagstone walkway. Hallett's descendants restored the house for use as a law office. His hotel was once home to fancy balls and cockfights; a functional rooster coop remains on the property.

Spear House
163 St. Emmanuel Street

Built in 1857, this red-brick, three-bay, side-hall townhouse features white stucco trim, cast-iron galleries, a wide bracketed overhang, and dentiled cornice, all of which suggest Italianate styling, although the construction date and square-headed windows evince Greek Revival influence. Narrow side yards and a shallow front yard remind one of Vieux Carré planning, while the small but lovely garden is vintage Mobile.

The Spear House is vintage Mobile mixed-style architecture—Italianate decoration but with square-headed windows and a construction prior to the commonly contemplated dates of the Italianate period.

Tardy Cottage
104 South Lawrence Street

This 3,400-square-foot raised, center–hall, five-bay Gulf Coast cottage with Greek Revival detailing was constructed in 1858 by auctioneer and commission merchant Balthazar Tardy. It exhibits perfect classical simplicity, with Tuscan posts, pedimented dormers with pilasters and six-over-six lights, and a gallery with a wood rail. A double stairway, added later, leads to an entrance with a transom extending over the door and sidelights. The first floor, once inhabited by slaves, is brick, while the second story is wood frame, stuccoed and scored to resemble stone.

Tardy Cottage's double stairway leading to the front-elevation gallery is unique to the Mobile area in the raised-cottage type, although the feature was common on the Mississippi Gulf Coast prior to Hurricane Katrina.

Guesnard House
51 South Jackson Street

Tobacconist, jeweler, and incorporator of the "Can't Get Away Club," an organization providing relief to plague sufferers, Theodore Guesnard, Jr., hired architect David Cumming, Jr., and builders James Hill and James Robertson to construct this two-story, red-brick Italianate townhouse with two-story wings in 1855. The cast-iron gallery and fence and sawtooth dentil course beneath a bracketed overhanging cornice are indicative of the style, but square-headed windows with six-over-nine double-hung sashes and the pilastered entrance with acanthus-scrolled corbels beneath the lintel point to its construction during the Greek Revival era. A Guesnard daughter married state senator John Kraft, "father of the Alabama highway system," and resided here from 1919 to 1935. The house was acquired by the Government Street Presbyterian Church in 1965.

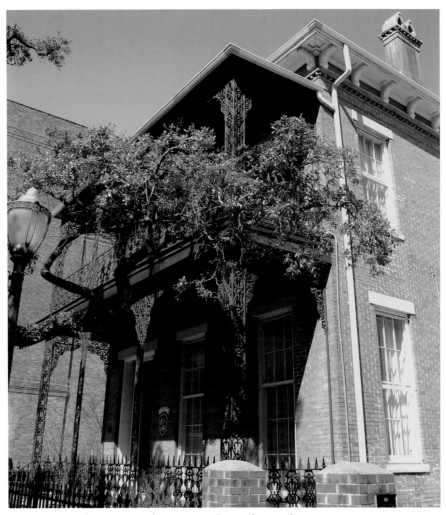

The Guesnard House, with its rare side garden and impressive interior, is open to tours by appointment.

The front parlor features fourteen-foot-high ceilings, walnut and gold cornices with matching pier glasses, and original pine floors .

Guesnard House offers unique window treatments.

This white marble mantel is located in the front parlor.

The dining room is graced by an Italian marble mantel and a gas chandelier of brass (now electrified), which is original to the house. Church members needlepointed the chair cushions.

A curving mahogany staircase leads from the Guesnard House's foyer to the second floor.

Hamilton House
407 Church Street

Attorney Thomas A. Hamilton, instrumental in having the ship channel in Mobile Bay dredged, built this mixed-style, two-story, brick townhouse in 1859. Although the arched cast-iron gallery with floral motifs is of the Italianate style, the flat-headed full-length windows, steep gable roof with double chimneys at the ends, and pilastered entrance with acanthus-scrolled corbels beneath the lintel are classical elements. The house was converted to business use in 1934 but was restored in 1967 to a family residence by Mrs. Edwin K. Smith.

Hamilton House has a distinctive arched, cast-iron gallery.

Big Zion A.M.E. Church
112 Bayou Street

The congregation of what is now the Big Zion African Methodist Episcopal Church originated in 1842 with a group of slaves worshiping in their master's Methodist church. They erected a structure here in 1868 under the name Little Zion but in 1895 remodeled the church and renamed it Big Zion, to reflect its increasing religious and cultural significance to its congregants. The remodeling was in the Romanesque style, replete with a basilical plan, stuccoed façade with arched windows, and projecting square towers. However, the pointed traceried windows with hood molding in the second story's central bay are pure Gothic Revival. In 1865, Zion A.M.E. Church became the first church in Mobile to have an African-American minister, Rev. Ferdinand Smith, be ordained by a black bishop.

Zion A.M.E. Church was the first Mobile church to have an African-American minister ordained by a black bishop.

The Zion parsonage, next door at 110 Bayou Street, was erected for $11,000 in 1908. The George Rogers design features Mediterranean influences, such as stucco and a tile roof. The double gallery is supported by Tuscan columns and has a second-story wood railing.

Ketchum House
400 Government Street

Built in 1860 by architect Thomas James for Confederate major William H. Ketchum, this three-story brick mansion was occupied during the Civil War by U.S. general E. R. S. Canby, although Mrs. Ketchum refused eviction and remained in the home. The asymmetrical massing; heavily bracketed eaves decorated with modillions; white stone quoins; arched cast-iron galleries ornamented with grape meanders, arabesques, and geometric patterns; stringcourses between the stories; and paired second-story windows indicate the Italianate style. The interior features rooms distinguished by molded-plaster friezes, ceiling medallions of camellias and magnolias, Tiffany glass chandeliers, and a spiral staircase reaching the third story.

Ketchum House has twenty-three rooms, including a sixty-square-foot drawing room that covers the entire third floor. Since 1906, it has housed the bishop of the Catholic Diocese of Mobile.

Frohlichstein/Goldsmith Houses
357-59 Church Street

Bavarian immigrants, brothers-in-law, and dry-goods business partners William Frolichstein and Isaac Goldsmith built these two-story, mixed-style, side-hall-plan twin houses in 1862 for their families. Abraham Pincus acquired them in 1888, and his descendants resided here for seventy-five years. Mardi Gras parades have begun and ended at this courtyard for decades. Italianate-style elements include arched cast-iron galleries and bracketed cornices of the facing side wings and the recessed connecting building, although the square-headed openings, rectangular transom and sidelights framing the entrances, and interior side-hall plans are typical of classical design.

Since 1967, the Frohlichstein/Goldsmith Houses have served as a fashionable B&B called the Malaga Inn, replete with marble mantels, gold-leaf pier glasses, crystal chandeliers, and three-story addition.

51

Arched cast-iron galleries grace the buildings.

One of the original parlors of the house serves as a gathering place for guests of the Malaga Inn.

This guestroom, like others in the house, is decorated with antiques, including a four-poster bed.

An upstairs guestroom catches warm afternoon sunlight through a diamond-shaped, single-color, stained-glass window.

The courtyard's central fountain, surrounded on all sides by two floors of guestrooms, serves as an outdoor gathering place for the inn. Mardi Gras parades begin and end at the courtyard's street-side entrance.

Horst House
407 Conti Street

This two-story, five-bay, brick center-hall structure was designed in the Italianate style, as evidenced by the bracketed overhanging eaves with paneled parapet, cornice with carved modillions in scroll design with pendants and brick dentil course, segmental-arched windows with curved cast-iron lintels crowned by an anthemion, one-story three-bay cast-iron porch with delicately latticed posts, and spandrels and frieze decorated with leafy rinceau and arabesque patterns. It was erected in 1867 at a cost of $26,000 by London-born master mason George Cox for Martin Horst. Restored in 1971 as a restaurant, it currently serves as law offices.

The Horst House was included in the National Register of Historic Places in 1971. Its nickname, "Moongate," derives from its round gate, added that same year.

The segmental-arched windows reflect the Italianate design.

Pollock House
501 Government Street

Merchant Jacob Pollock commissioned this Italianate townhouse in 1876, and his descendants maintain ownership today. The asymmetrical massing, low-hipped roof, cornice with bracketed overhanging eaves decorated with twin acanthus-scrolled modillions, castiron balustrade above a bay window, diamond-paned sash with one-over-one lights, pronounced quoins, pilasters, and arched recessed entrance are indicative of the late Italianate style. The matching ironwork of the fence and balcony are typical of this grand era in Mobile.

The Pollock House's iron gate, decorated with trefoil and wheel motifs in a geometric framework, is a pleasing addition to the cast-iron fence on the front elevation.

Lower Dauphin Historic District

Cathedral of the Immaculate Conception
4 South Claiborne Street

The cornerstone for this Italian Renaissance-style structure was laid in 1835. The main building, designed by Claude Beroujon with a forty-foot-high pilastered side elevation and ten-foot-thick brick walls replete with granite keystones and arched windows, was finally completed in 1849. The cast-iron fence and classical hexastyle portico, with Roman Doric columns and a denticulated triangular pediment, were begun by architect James F. Hutchinson in 1875 and finished by his son of the same name in 1887. The younger Hutchinson also completed the two front-elevation towers in 1895, one of which was struck by an airplane in 1947. German stained-glass windows were added in the 1890s.

This cathedral was begun in 1835, dedicated in 1850, and designated a minor basilica by Pope John XXIII in 1962. It is located in the Lower Dauphin Historic District, which was listed in the National Register of Historic Places in 1979. During a 2003 renovation of the cathedral's interior, Carrara marble floors were installed in the main and side aisles.

The fountains in this parklike setting on Cathedral Square are a popular Mobile spot day or night, but especially with the backdrop of the cathedral's stunning nighttime lighting.

The cathedral's nave has a magnificent vaulted ceiling. The building has survived an explosion (1865), airplane hit (1947), fire (1954), and numerous hurricanes.

Bishop John L. May renovated the sanctuary and altar in the 1970s, moving the altar forward, adding a bronze representation of Christ, and placing a large crucifix over the tabernacle.

Twelve stained-glass windows, measuring thirty feet by twelve feet and depicting New Testament themes, were made in Munich by Franz Mayer Company.

Underneath the center of the main floor, down a spiral staircase, is a crypt for the burial of bishops.

Detonti Square Historic District

Hunter-King House
259 North Conception Street

This one-and-a-half-story frame Gulf Coast cottage was built in 1836 as a basic square cottage with a gable roof and porch with four square posts and simple molded capitals. Renovations made later that century included the addition of rear wings and two Greek Revival dormers with fluted pilasters. The simple round-rail gallery balustrade, full-length shuttered windows, window-door-door-window façade alignment, and square-headed openings are indicative of the purer Gulf Coast cottage type.

The Hunter-King House was erected in the vernacular Gulf Coast cottage style, without Greek Revival elements such as a center-hall plan or classical-order columns.

Beal-McNeal House
205 North Conception Street

Old Spring Hill developer Gustavus Beal hired B. Davenport to build this one-story, five-bay frame Gulf Coast cottage raised on fourteen courses of brick piers in 1836, likely according to Beal's own design. Beal descended from the Vine and Olive Colony, a settlement of Napoleonic refugees in Demopolis, Alabama. This cottage was later reoriented so the gable end would face the street. The result is a complete Greek temple appearance, with a pediment and heavy entablature, six fluted cypress Doric columns, simple wood rail, and six-over-six lights. This is a good example of the Greek Revival-style cottage in Mobile.

Recently renovated by Robert Hunter, the Beal-McNeal House is part of the Detonti Square Historic District, which was added to the National Register of Historic Places in 1972.

Turner Cottage
305 State Street

This raised Gulf Coast cottage was built in 1836 by Jesse Turner, sold in 1841 to pharmacist Dr. Richard L. Watkins, and subsequently acquired by the Suck sisters. In 1973, it was purchased by the Mobile Historic Development Commission for restoration. The type is evident in the frame structure raised on brick piers, gable roof with no overhang, dormers with curved lintels, and pilastered floor-length windows opening onto a gallery with Tuscan columns. The center-hall, double-parlor interior design shows a Greek Revival influence.

The Turner Cottage is a good example of the mixed-style Gulf Coast cottage with Greek Revival elements.

Parmly Houses
303-5-7 North Conception Street

Dentist Ludolph Parmly had the two-and-a-half-story red-brick houses built at 303 and 305 North Conception Street in the Federal style in 1842, replete with gable roofs, dormers, and box galleries. He endowed the 305 house with a cast-iron gallery after 1850. In 1852, Dr. Parmly built a third house at 307, a three-story, brick, side-hall residence sufficient to accommodate his expanding family. The third house is Greek Revival style, with double-hung sashes with six-over-six lights.

The Parmly Houses represent a movement from Federal to Greek Revival style, especially with the detailing evident in the openings.

The third house features a recessed classical entrance with transom and sidelights, slightly pedimented Greek key trim, and massive battered pilasters.

Gee-Pugh House
251 St. Anthony Street

Built in 1852 by cabinetmaker Gideon Gee at 253 Monroe Street, the two-story, red-brick Gee House was moved in 1969 to the Detonti Square Historic District to make way for the expanding Interstate Highway 10. Originally a Federal-style building, when resurrected on St. Anthony Street it was altered by the addition of an iron gallery with batten shutters and the raising of the gable end walls. It is currently home to a political organization.

The Gee-Pugh House has a gable roof with asphalt shingles and a service wing that survived its move from Monroe Street. The relocation demonstrates the exceptional commitment made by Mobilians to preserve their architectural history.

St. John House
201 North Conception Street

City councilman and cotton land baron Thomas St. John built this two-story, three-bay, fifteen-room masonry townhouse in 1857. It features a low-hipped roof supported by heavy wooden brackets, cornice with wreath designs centered between the brackets, cast-iron gallery with iron posts and gallery floor, and front steps crafted of white marble. A major financial supporter of the Confederacy, St. John saw his wife's likeness, knitting socks for Rebel soldiers, printed upon a Confederate banknote.

The Italianate-style St. John House was occupied by the original owner's descendants until 1968, when it was restored by Mr. and Mrs. Borden Strickland.

Richards House
256 North Joachim Street

Maine native and riverboat captain Charles Richards built this side-hall Italianate townhouse in 1860, with widely overhanging eaves, polygonal bays, gray and white marble squares adorning the front-porch floor, and a walkway composed of flagstones that formerly decorated the downtown area. The cast-iron gallery features "Four Seasons" figures and foliated arabesques, while the entrance transom and sidelights contain etched Bohemian leaded glass. Renovated by the Ideal Cement Company in 1946-47 and used as office space until donated to the city in 1972, the house is now a city-owned museum and headquarters of Daughters of the American Revolution.

The Richards House is a vintage example of Mobile's Italianate style, with a low roof, wide overhang, and exemplary cast-iron gallery. The interior features medallions in the plaster ceilings, original Carrara marble mantels, bronze chandeliers in the double parlor, a Baccarat crystal chandelier in the dining room, and a curved front-hall staircase.

The front porch iron railing features a four seasons design.

This black chandelier is by Christian Cornelius of Philadelphia.

The dining room features a Carrara marble mantel with mirror.

The 1880 Weber piano was owned by Richards.

Richards House offers a lovely curving staircase in the entry hall.

Lyon House
261 North Joachim Street

This mixed-style, two-story, brick townhouse was erected in 1859 by cotton broker Thomas Temple Armstrong Lyon, although the offset polygonal bay left of the main façade is a later addition. The entrance and fenestration are Greek Revival style, although the arched, projecting, two-story, three-bay, cast-iron gallery, which is painted white and features trellises, a frieze, and balustrade, constitutes Italianate decoration. The white lintels and sills contrast with the red-brick walls in a manner often utilized by architects who favor the Federal style.

A pair of wrought-iron gates from the estate of Lewis Carroll (author of Alice's Adventures in Wonderland) *further distinguishes Lyon House.*

Butt-Kling House
254 North Jackson Street

C. W. Butt, son of the architect who built Christ Episcopal Church, erected this Italianate-style house in 1861. It features a projecting front bay, stone quoins at every angle, low-hipped roof, and overhanging cornice decorated with scrolled brackets and black modillions. The Kling family, of the Mobile Kling Iron Foundry, owned the structure from 1899 to 1966. Julian McGowins restored it in 1969. The recessed, single-bay, cast-iron rail is not original.

The Butt-Kling House has an ironwork entranceway that matches the ironwork fencing.

The Butt-Kling House features an impressive projecting front bay.

Bush-Sands Memorial
254 St. Anthony Street

Cotton factor John Bush built this three-bay, Italianate-style house in 1868, with a Renaissance-style entrance framed by paneled pilasters, carved acanthus brackets, and a transom and sidelights made of Bohemian leaded, beveled glass. The bracketed cornice with parapet above and the second-story cast-iron gallery supported by narrow posts with neo-Corinthian capitals reveal the house's Italianate style. Bush's descendant, Sarah Bush, willed the property to her granddaughter, Willie Bush. The latter married and resided in this house with Dr. Gerald Mohr, the Confederate scientist, author, and physician who fought then-misunderstood malaria in Mobile by advocating the inoculation of children and the equipping of houses with screens. His ideas prompted some to stone his carriage as it passed them on the streets.

The Bush-Sands Memorial now serves as headquarters for Mobile's oldest parading mystic society, the Order of Mystics.

The otherwise hidden L shape of the rear creates a unique courtyard. Both shuttered and open porches and balconies are framed by wisteria in the spring.

Oakleigh Garden Historic District

Oakleigh Place
350 Oakleigh Street

South Carolina native and brickyard owner James W. Roper erected this *T*-shaped Greek Revival-style mansion in 1833 using slave labor. It is situated on former plantation lands that were included in a Spanish land grant known as the Farve Tract. Although Roper was forced to quitclaim the house to the Bank of the United States during the Panic of 1837 in payment of a $20,000 debt, he was allowed to reside here until 1848. A frame second story rises from a brick ground level, and an exterior, curved, wooden staircase leads to an upper gallery that is supported by square Doric pillars. Mobile socialites Alfred and Margaret Irwin purchased the house in 1852. Now headquarters to the Historic Mobile Preservation Society, it is open to the public.

Oakleigh Place was listed in National Register of Historic Places in 1971 and is the centerpiece of the Oakleigh Garden Historic District, which was listed in the register in 1972.

The graceful, curved, front-gallery staircase features a round-top railing.

This parlor is furnished with a period portrait, writing table, secretary, and black marble mantel over an original coal-burning fireplace.

Oakleigh's second parlor, with a white marble mantel and Federal mirror and chandelier, is also a music room with a box grand piano.

The first-floor dining room has heart-pine flooring.

The master bedroom, known as the Batre Room, features a wallpaper pattern based on a swatch from a White House gown worn by Martha Washington. Daisy Roper was friends with Mrs. Washington's granddaughter.

Cox-Deasy House
1115 Palmetto Street

The third-oldest house in the Oakleigh Garden Historic District, this Greek Revival three-bay cottage was constructed in 1850 by master builder and brick mason George Cox, who also erected the Horst House and Rapelje-Delaney House. The gallery supported by four Doric posts and the entrance with rectangular sidelights and transom exemplify the style, while the full-length French doors were a popular Mobile idiom of the era.

The Cox family retained ownership of Cox-Deasy House until they willed it to the Historic Mobile Preservation Society in 1977.

The rear elevation, with a wing for servants or additional family, looks onto a courtyard and garden.

Rapelje-Delaney House (Landmark Hall)
1005 Government Street

This house was built by master mason George Cox for Astoria, New York native and cotton broker George Rapelje in 1865 and sold for $25,000 four years later. George Rogers modified it in 1906 for Dr. O. F. Cawthon. The three-story, twenty-nine-room, five-bay, center-hall mansion is in the Greek and Renaissance Revival style. It is notable for its projecting three-bay, double-gallery side porch and two-bay rear porch. The front elevation features Greek key door trim, marble quoins, an overhanging and dentiled cornice bracketed with plain beam ends, stuccoed and scored façade, one-story gallery with balustrade, and narrow Tuscan columns.

The Rapelje-Delaney House is notable for its projecting side porch.

The Rapelje-Delaney House features distinctly styled side and rear elevations.

The Rapelje-Delaney House interior is distinguished by sixteen-foot-high ceilings and marble windowsills. During the 1906 renovation, the dining room walls were covered with a Japanese paper embossed with oxidized silver figures.

The drawing room features a magnificent mantel, equestrian statue, and inlaid marble floor.

The interior is distinguished by stained woods, utilized for ceiling beams, the staircase foundation, railings and banisters, and handmade moldings.

The landing of the oak staircase features a stained-glass window with the family crest.

One of few original structures in Mobile, the carriage house is tucked at the back of the deep lot on Government Street, far from the main house.

Hellen House
1001 Augusta Street

This mixed Italianate/Greek Revival, three-bay, side-hall building was constructed in 1869-70 for Mariah H. Hellen and purchased in 1876 by Maj. Stephens Croom, whose descendants owned it into the twenty-first century. The two-story portico is supported by full-length square Tuscan columns, aligned with twin brackets under the eaves. Shuttered windows with six-over-six lights adorn the façade, and the twin balustrades were cut from flat boards in multiple two-dimensional patterns.

The renovated Hellen House has a stair hall beside double parlors, a Mobile plan since the 1850s. The building is a fine example of Mobile's bracketed Italianate style, with full-height, square, neoclassical columns echoed by paired brackets above each.

Goelete-Randlette House
1005 Augusta Street

Virginia and Edward Goelete constructed this one-and-a-half-story, wood-frame, Greek Revival-style, raised cottage in 1868 and sold it in 1875 to Columbia E. Randlette and William Randlette, the captain of the schooner *Monactico*. They added two parlors on the east side in 1880, making the house symmetrical with five bays, including a center hall. An entrance with a rectangular, leaded-glass transom and sidelights, wood railing, and six square Tuscan columns resting on molded bases and low square plinths highlight the classical styling of this side-gable cottage.

The Goelete-Randlette House, restored in 1968, has striking interior features, such as a stairway with walnut panels and turned balusters and a wood mantel in every room.

Roberts-Abbott House
910 Government Street

A vintage example of the Greek Revival style, this two-story, double-galleried, side-hall, frame house with central block and west wing was erected in 1855 by Joel Roberts. A rear was wing added by 1904 and an east wing by 1925. Four fluted Doric columns grace each gallery, while a triangular pediment with entablature and classically detailed fenestration and entranceway add to the simple Greek Revival elegance.

The Roberts-Abbott House's double gallery is typical of Mobile's Greek Revival architecture. A porch with full-height columns is more popular in eastern Alabama.

Porch ceilings are painted light blue for heat and insect control.

Joe Cain House
906 Augusta Street

Although American Mardi Gras parading as we know it originated in Mobile in 1831 with Michael Krafft's Cowbellion de Rakin Society, the revelry died out during the Civil War. Joe Cain revived the festival in 1867 by donning Chickasaw dress, anointing himself "Chief Slacabamorinico," and whooping through Mobile's streets on a charcoal wagon with six other similarly attired revelers. By 1872, Joe Cain's faith was rewarded with a fully restored Mobile Mardi Gras and membership in the venerable Order of Mystics. His father, Philadelphia native Joe Cain, built this classically influenced, three-bay, frame cottage in 1859. It features a three-bay porch with four Doric posts and a pierced gable.

Joe Cain, "the heart and soul of Mobile Mardi Gras," died in 1904 secure in the knowledge that Mardi Gras had endured and thrived in Mobile, and today the Joe Cain House is ground zero during one day's celebration every Carnival season.

A likeness of Mardi Gras king Joe Cain, portraying his fictional parading character, Chickasaw chief Slacabamorinico, appears on the house-number sign, along a Mardi Gras parade route.

Twelve Oaks (Smith-Cutts House)
250 Chatham Street

James Little and Virginia Alabama Smith built this two-bay, side-hall home in 1867-68 farther back on this property. In 1938, the Hays family moved it to its present location (sans its original two-story galleries) and restored it as "Twelve Oaks." A low-hipped roof with asphalt shingles, a full entablature and box cornice, square-headed full-length windows with four-over-six lights, gallery supported by massive box columns, and classically detailed entrance with transom and sidelights are elements of the house's predominantly Greek Revival style.

Iron-lace-decorated windows and century-old peach trees heighten the ambiance of the Twelve Oaks property. The house was recently restored.

Kilduff House
200 George Street

Architect J. F. Hutchisson designed this Gothic Revival-style raised cottage, which builder B. Sissaman erected in 1891 at a cost of $1,800. Raised on brick piers, the house features a projecting three-bay gallery with a flat roof and flat-cut balusters. Paired slender colonnettes with capitals, carved wooden panels forming arches between the columns, and flat-cut jigsaw work running along the raking cornices and eaves make this house unique in Mobile.

Kilduff House has a deep front lawn with camellias, great oaks, and a recently added white picket fence festooned with flowers.

Bennett House
1123 Church Street

John and Lula Bennett built this neoclassical-style, two-story, three-bay, side-hall, masonry house raised on twelve courses of brick piers in 1896. It features four full-length monumental wood box columns, a deeply pitched roof with dentiled cornice, frame porch, and arched windows with corresponding arched masonry lintels. A one-story brick rear wing has a low-hipped roof and slate shingles.

The Bennett House's overall appearance is reminiscent of the simplicity of earlier classical styles.

Blacksher Hall
1056 Government Street

Erected in 1900 by architect Rudolph Benz for cotton factor and commission merchant Charles T. Hearin, this Neoclassical Revival brick house has a triangular pediment, frieze decorated with rope and swag, projecting first-floor wood portico with paired Ionic columns surmounted by a balustraded deck, flat-headed full-length windows, and a five-bay center-hall plan indicative of the style. John T. Blacksher acquired the mansion in 1907, and his family retained it until 1952, when it became the Abba (Shriner) Temple. It is currently a private residence.

Blacksher Hall offers a profusion of Corinthian and Ionic columns. The interior is distinguished by stained-glass skylights and oculars (oval windows) and five sets of pocket doors.

Blacksher Hall is brimming with stairs, including a grand staircase with mahogany newel posts and bridge.

The first-floor parlor has a chandelier hanging from the second floor through an opening in the ceiling. The main parlor leads to a library and an additional parlor.

A second-floor stained-glass skylight is viewed here from the first floor.

The dining room features a marble mantel, oil painting, and stained leaded glass above the doors to the porch.

Blacksher Hall's dining room has an unusual curved wall.

Forcheimer-Burke-Helmer House
950 Government Street

This rectangular Queen Anne-style house with a gable roof and right side-hall entry was built in 1897-98 by grocer Louis Forcheimer. It features irregular massing, a two-story round turret, dormers with colorful denticulated cornices, scrolled and decorated brackets, cupola, pigeon garret, and one-story porch replete with three pairs of slender pseudo-Corinthian columns and turned-wood balustrade surmounted by a balustraded deck.

The Forcheimer-Burke-Helmer House was acquired in 1913 by a prominent Mobile undertaker.

Tacon-Gordon-Tissington-Vitalo House
1216 Government Street

Henry Tacon, secretary and treasurer of the Mobile and Ohio and Bay Shore railways, erected this two-and-one-half-story, center-hall, Queen Anne mansion in 1901. It features a high-hipped roof and cross-gable slate shingles, irregular massing, broken rooflines, a gable dormer with paired Ionic columns, and a full-width front-gallery with balusters, spindle-work, and narrow fluted Ionic columns. The three-story tower has decorative frieze bands, a bracketed cornice, and bell roof with covered vents. The Gordon family acquired the house in 1907.

The Tacon-Gordon-Tissington-Vitalo House interior offers original mantels, ceiling rosettes, and parlors with pale-gray French-linen wallpaper with gold-embossed patterns. The three "courting parlors" were built for Tacon's three daughters, although one became a bedroom after World War II.

The Tacon-Gordon-Tissington-Vitalo House offers a staircase with dark rubbed wood enriched by paneling and a stained-glass window on the landing. A mantel and chandelier further enhance this lovely scene.

The rear hall features tiger-oak moldings and scrollwork. The ceiling lights are original to the house but moved from other rooms. Originally screening each door in the house, only one drapery panel remains; it reverses from gold to dark green.

An upstairs casual room features a pair of cane-back chairs and an unusually shaped leather-top writing desk.

Burgess-Maschmeyer House
1209 Government Street

Contractor E. S. Ward built this three-story, five-bay, gray-brick, Italian Renaissance-style house in 1906, pursuant to architect George Rogers' design for cotton merchant David R. Burgess. Elements of the style include the tile-covered hipped roof, wide overhanging eaves resting on paired brackets, paired Indiana limestone Tuscan columns supporting an eighty-four-foot-long wraparound porch, entrance and fenestration with fanlight transoms, terracotta trim, second-story central-bay arch, and masonry balustraded deck.

The Burgess House interior, designed by Cincinnatian William F. Behrens, features a Georgian entrance hall and three-story staircase with frescos and murals handpainted and signed (1907) by Thil Wilbergand, a sixteenth-century Italian Renaissance reception room, and a Tudor-style library. A circular-walled dining room with mahogany wainscoting and pilasters has framed painted panels of cherubs dancing with festoons of flowers.

The Burgess House affords the visitor a lovely view from the second-story balcony.

Old Dauphin Way Historic District

Vincent House
1664 Spring Hill Avenue

Capt. Benjamin Vincent, owner of the steamer packet *Bethlehem*, constructed this Louisiana plantation-style frame house (circa 1827) with brick piers, an impressive front stairway, and wood lap siding. His wife was sister to Michael Krafft, founder of Mobile's first Mardi Gras association, the Cowbellion de Rakin Society, and resident in this house for many years. Vincent sold it to pay his real-estate taxes, and a 1902 alteration designed by architect C. L. Hutchisson, Sr., enclosed the ground floor.

Also known as Walshwood, the Vincent House was again remodeled in 1927. Located on the campus of Mobile Children's Hospital, it houses a medical museum.

A side view shows the building's wood lap siding.

The rear elevation features an attractive garden.

This iron sculpture, Follow the Leader, *by W. Stanley Proctor, is on the grounds of the Geri Moulton Children's Park.*

Gates-Daves House
1570 Dauphin Street

This seven-bay, one-story, frame, plaster-fronted, Creole-influenced cottage was built by Hezekiah Gates in 1842. A long, narrow gallery sports chamfered columns and a swallowtail baluster cut. The full-length French doors lead into every room, including an entrance center hall, a decidedly Greek Revival notion. It was remodeled after 1878, resulting in the destruction of the rear wings, although the original brick wine cellar still lies under the west side. Mr. Alfred Daves, a descendant of Gates, later resided here.

The Gates-Daves House was listed in the National Register of Historic Places in 1974.

Macy House
1569 Dauphin Street

This two-story, frame, three-bay, Gothic Revival cottage was erected in 1867 for the R. C. Macy family. An architectural adaptation from Andrew J. Downing's Design XVI, "A Bracketed Farm-House of Wood," it features a hipped roof, board-and-batten siding, decorative bargeboards, pointed windows with hood molds, and gables with quatrefoil motifs and jigsaw-cut decorations. The porch has four chamfered posts connected by a cusped frieze.

Macy House is part of the Old Dauphin Way Historic District, Mobile's largest such neighborhood, which was listed in the National Register of Historic Places in 1984.

Many varieties of camellias, roses, and azaleas grace the Macy House grounds.

Macy House has a large backyard live oak with a rope swing.

Monterey Place
1552 Monterey Place

A marvelous example of Queen Anne-style architecture, this two-story, frame house with a pyramidal roof and projecting wings was built in 1897 by contractor J. P. Emrich for Charles M. Shepherd (whose descendants resided here until 1974) at a cost of $3,115, pursuant to a Rudolph Benz design. It has delicate spindles beneath upper and lower cornices, curving bargeboard decorating the first-floor gallery, irregularly massed gables, a single gabled east-side dormer, and a wide turret over a circular bay on the southwest corner. From 1910 to 1952, Miss Kitty Shepherd's School occupied the second floor.

Monterey Place, also known as Shepherd House, was listed in the National Register of Historic Places in 1984. Miss Shepherd's great-uncles were Mississippi governor John T. McRae and Confederate chief financial officer Colin McRae.

Monterey Place offers an impressive front-elevation gable.

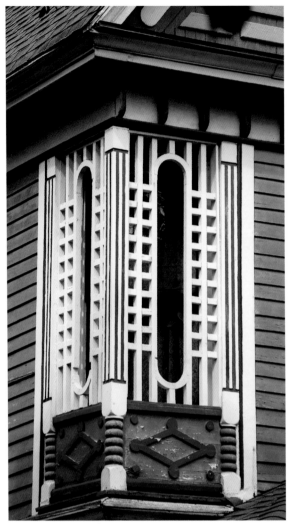

Bright colors dominate the exterior molding and detail work, including this front corner window.

Monterey Place has a dramatic turret as a key part of its Queen Anne-style elements.

Midtown Historic District

Carlen House
54 South Carlen

This one-and-a-half-story, five-bay, frame, Gulf Coast raised cottage was erected in 1843 by farmer Michael Carlen for his Irish bride. It occupies part of the Dubroca Tract of the 1804 Spanish land grant. The cottage has a steeply pitched roof, plastered-over heavy-pegged framing, clapboard siding, and numerous Greek Revival elements such as six box columns with Tuscan capitals, a four-panel door flanked by pilasters, and a center-hall plan opening onto a rear gallery. Owned by the Carlen family until 1923, the house was later purchased by the Mobile County School Board.

The Carlen House, restored by architect Nicholas Holmes, was listed in the National Register of Historic Places in 1981.

Georgia Cottage
2564 Spring Hill Avenue

This Greek Revival-style raised cottage was built in 1845 by Virginia-born cotton factor William A. Hardaway and his wife, Mary J. Delbarco, possibly with slave labor. It was later the residence of Confederate sympathizer and novelist Augusta Jane Evans (*St. Elmo, Beulah,* and *Macaria*) and the family of Dr. Edwards S. and Mary Sledge. The house has a hipped roof and cypress framing, a five-bay verandah with box columns, and a plastered façade. An oak-lined driveway offers a dramatic welcome to approaching visitors.

Georgia Cottage, also known as the Hardaway House, was listed in the National Register of Historic Places in 1972. It was the boyhood home of E. B. Sledge, author of the World War II memoir With the Old Breed.

Georgia Cottage offers an Old South favorite, an oak alley.

Bragg-Mitchell House
1906 Spring Hill Avenue

Mobile architect Thomas S. James likely designed this fourteen-room, *T*-shaped, bracketed Greek Revival mansion amidst a live-oak grove in 1855 for North Carolina native and co-drafter of the Confederate Constitution, Judge John Bragg. His brother, Confederate general Braxton Bragg, was a frequent visitor to this house. The second-story box gallery, square-headed windows, and Greek key framing of interior doors are typical elements of the classical style, while the scrolled, bracketed cornice and slender form of the sixteen fluted Doric columns are specifically indicative of the bracketed Greek Revival style.

The Bragg-Mitchell House was listed in the National Register of Historic Places in 1972 and is open to the public during seasonal tours and other occasions.

The live oaks grew from the acorns of the original oaks lost during the Civil War.

The Bragg-Mitchell House has a ballroom with dramatic arches and columns fashioned in the Italianate style.

Judge Bragg's twenty-four-karat-gold mirrors were purchased in New York City.

This sideboard, one of the few surviving furnishings once owned by Judge Bragg, was spared from his otherwise unsuccessful efforts to hide valuables from invading Union Army pilferers.

Sacred Heart Chapel
2300 Spring Hill Avenue

This Richardsonian Romanesque Revival chapel in the Greek-cross plan was erected in 1894, one year before its dedication. It was designed by New Orleans architects Harrod and Andry and built by Louisville contractors M. T. Newman and Company, with Herman Brunns as the construction architect. This massive stone structure has walls of rusticated limestone and granite, and the gable is distinguished by gargoyles at its ends and is crowned by a heavy stone cross.

Thanks to a gift by the McGill family, Sacred Heart Chapel at the Visitation Monastery is now an oratory open to the public.

This arched front entrance is crafted in the Romanesque Revival style with rusticated stone. The cornerstone was blessed on January 29, 1894; the chapel dedicated in 1895.

A former school was converted into the Convent of the Visitation's retreat complex.

The Sacred Heart Chapel sanctuary has alabaster vases and marble altars. The tabernacle is to the right, and the top-center relief shows Jesus appearing to Saint Margaret Mary, asking for adoration of the Blessed Sacrament.

Sacred Heart Chapel's nave has stained-glass windows donated by convent benefactors. The middle scene is called "Jesus Blessing the Children."

Spring Hill Neighborhood

Collins-Robinson House
56 Oakland Avenue

Robert Bunker, president of the Southern Life Assurance and Trust Company, likely erected this one-and-a-half-story raised Gulf Coast cottage with frame construction and clapboard siding in 1830 with a hall and two rooms, but it appears that the Collins family made substantial alterations in 1843. Elizabeth Marston purchased it in 1870 and built two more rooms, and her family added two dormers in the early 1900s. The five-bay, center-hall structure has a steeply pitched gable roof, a stairway leading to a double-leaf front door, a gallery with box columns with molded capitals, and a simple wood balustrade.

The Collins-Robinson House, located in the fashionable Spring Hill subdivision, was originally built as a country home outside the city limits of Mobile.

Beal-Galliard House
111 Myrtlewood Lane

Developer Gustavus Beal erected this raised Gulf Coast cottage in 1836 in what was then the village of Spring Hill, a summer retreat for plague- and heat-weary Mobilians. The heavy-pegged framing, plastered façade, six-foot-wide paneled cypress door with English brass hardware, gallery with six chamfered posts, round-top railing, gable roof, French doors, and sixteen-foot-high ceilings are elements of the early country-house type. Lawyer Samuel Palmer Galliard purchased the home in 1903 as a gift for his wife, Maddie. He enlarged the north wing and added the south rear wing.

Beal-Galliard House was named to the National Register of Historic Places in 1984. A Carpenter Gothic guest cottage, giant oaks, azaleas, and dogwoods grace this property in addition to the impressive main house.

Carolina Hall
70 South McGregor Avenue

Former Charleston resident and cotton factor William Dawson built this two-story, three-bay, double-galleried house in 1845. This bracketed Greek Revival-style residence has fluted columns with Tower of Winds capitals (with a row of acanthus leaves below a circle of water leaves), decorative balustrades on both levels, a Greek key door, and a triangular pediment with denticulated cornices. It was acquired in 1914 by the Perdue family and given the name "Yester House" but had its original name restored by subsequent owners Dr. and Mrs. Louis C. Wilson.

The Carolina Hall interior was modified by architect George Rogers for the F. A. Luling family after 1883. It features round and rectangular plasterwork ceiling medallions, crown molding with acanthus-leaf and egg-and-dart patterns, and fluted pilasters and columns dividing double parlors. The house was added to the National Register of Historic Places in 1973.

The dining room features fluted Corinthian columns and pilasters.

Near Carolina Hall's enclosed rear gallery, curved stairs lead to the second floor.

Stewartfield
Spring Hill College

This Greek Revival-style raised cottage with two side wings was built in 1850 by Scottish cotton factor Roger Stewart and his Irish wife, Isabella. It features a pyramidal roof, five-bay gallery with six fluted Doric columns and front steps leading to a Greek key door entrance with a transom and sidelights framed by pilasters. It also has jib windows, which slide up into the wall, with hinged wooden panels below the sash that can be opened when the sash slides up, creating a door to the porch. In addition to the rear semicircular ballroom, the house originally came with a now-defunct large oval racetrack in front, but the inspiring oak alley between the track and house still welcomes visitors in grand antebellum style. The house name is an amalgamation of the names of owners Stewart and Anna S. Field.

Stewartfield was added to the National Register of Historic Places in 1984. It was remodeled in 1930 by Mabel Byrne. The elegant interior includes marble fireplaces in the parlors and a center hall replete with chandeliers and ceiling medallions.

Stewartfield offers a vintage Old South tradition—a central hall.

Stewartfield has one of Mobile's two outstanding oak alleys.

Marshall-Eslava-Hixon-Dixon House
152 Tuthill Lane

Surrounded by a garden landscaped by his German wife and anchored by a front urn and stuccoed brick basin, this one-story, Greek Revival-style, center-hall house was built in 1853 by cotton factor and realtor Benjamin Franklin Marshall, a native of South Carolina. The raised-basement structure is of pegged-frame construction and features a hipped roof, a dentiled cornice, a stuccoed façade, a balustraded gallery supported by six fluted Doric columns, and an entrance flanked by Ionic colonnettes. The Jerome Eslava family owned this house for forty-five years.

The Marshall-Dixon House stands on land that was once the site of an 1828 frame church and a graveyard. The interior is highlighted by Greek key doors (with battered jambs and eared architraves) and crown molding with dentil courses.

Palmetto Hall

55 South McGregor Avenue

This center-hall mansion was erected in 1850 by John Dawson as a replica of his Charleston home, "Azalea Grove." The Greek Revival-style, three-bay, first-floor gallery is stuccoed and supported by plastered-masonry Tuscan pillars, while the Federal-style, five-bay, second-story gallery has six wooden, fluted Doric columns; a full-length balustrade; a fanlight transom; and wood siding. Jay P. Altmayer redesigned the interior in 1963 with a monumental stair hall and classic-baroque detailing and renamed it "Palmetto Hall."

Palmetto Hall's graceful magnolia trees and azaleas were added during the McKeon ownership (1922-60).

Saint Paul's Episcopal Chapel
4051 Old Shell Road

A vintage example of Carpenter Gothic style, this white board-and-batten frame chapel was designed and constructed in 1859 by John Dawson and Albert Stein (the engineer responsible for the city waterworks), aided by black craftsmen. It was consecrated in 1861 by rector J. Nichols and Mississippi's first bishop, William Mercer Green, although the original bell was not placed in the belfry until 1903. The wood-post gallery shades round-headed windows, with tracery forming lancets filled with diamond-shaped glass panes.

Saint Paul's Episcopal Chapel was named to the National Register of Historic Places in 1984.

Ashland Place Historic District

Waterman House
2254 Deleon Avenue

Mobile architect George Rogers designed this wood-frame, two-story, Colonial Revival house in 1908 for John B. Waterman. The three-bay first floor features Doric columns and fanlight transoms over two windows, and the four-bay second story has a balustraded deck, leaded-glass windows, and three pedimented dormers with arched fanlight transoms.

Waterman House is part of the Ashland Place Historic District, which was listed in the National Register of Historic Places in 1987.

Leinkauf Historic District

Chamberlain House
211 Michigan Avenue

This raised, two-story, five-bay house with irregular massing, wood siding, and complex gable roof was constructed for Herschel R. Glass in 1899 in the Queen Anne style. Additional elements of the style include gable bargeboards, asphalt shingles, a gabled one-story front porch, and a gabled balcony over the front porch. A single-leaf oak door with a decorative surround and transom, a widow's walk with square posts and turned spindles, and one-over-one double-hung sash windows with louvered shutters complete the cohesive design.

Chamberlain House is located in the Leinkauf Historic District, named to the National Register of Historic Places in 1987.

Downtown

Caravello House
7 North Jackson Avenue

Louise Caravello had this two-and-a-half-story, four-bay, brick townhouse constructed in 1835 with a millinery-shop entrance on the right and living quarters upstairs. A middle window was later reconfigured as the entrance and a second-story balcony replaced. Federal-style details include the gable roof; cornice with dentil course; and two dormers (front and rear) with double sashes, upper lights curved in a shallow segmental arch, and framed with fluted pilasters.

The Caravello House was named to the National Register of Historic Places in 1982. It was one of the few similar brick townhouses in the area to survive an 1839 fire. It is currently a print shop.

Martin Luther King, Jr. Area

Dave Patton House
1252 Martin Luther King, Jr. Avenue

African-American contractor and real-estate speculator Dave Patton built this two-story frame mansion in 1915. It features a full-width front porch supported by large brick piers and a two-story side porch/porte-cochere on the east elevation. The second-story porch is balustraded, with a molded handrail and turned decorative balusters. The interior is decorated in the Craftsman and classical styles. Patton proved a great success in Mobile until his early death in 1927 at age forty-seven. One of his major contracts involved providing some of his forty mules for mystic organization parades during Mardi Gras.

The Dave Patton House was purchased from the Patton family in 1979 for use as the parsonage for the Stewart Memorial C.M.E. Church. It was added to the National Register of Historic Places in 1987 and is on the African American Heritage Trail of Mobile.

Daphne

Adams-Stone House
907 Captain O'Neal Drive

This five-bay, Gulf Coast cottage raised on twenty-nine piers and set atop a bluff overlooking Mobile Bay was built in 1850 for Capt. James Adams, pilot of the 145-ton *Cahawba* steamboat. He entertained Pres. Millard Fillmore here that same year. Greek Revival elements include a center-hall plan; a simple entablature; a side gable roof; engaged pilasters at both ends of the façade; pedimented dormers; jib windows with six-over-six lights; an entrance with a four-panel door, shoulder architrave, sidelights, and transom; and a porch with balustrade and boxed columns with capitals that is approached by a central stair with square newels.

The Adams-Stone House retains two outbuildings from a bygone era, but the screens and glass enclosing the front and rear porches were added in 1976.